Passing on our Fe

to Children in their early years

Some thoughts and prayers for family and friends
at the time of Baptism and later

Jenny Pate

Illustrated by William Webb

McCrimmons
Great Wakering, Essex, England

The following themes indicated (*) stem from the active moments of parents and others in the ceremony of Baptism.

Contents

First published in the United Kingdom in 2001 by
McCrimmon Publishing Co. Ltd.,
Great Wakering, Essex, England
email: mccrimmons@dial.pipex.com
website: www.mccrimmons.com

Text © 2001 Jenny Pate
Design and layout © 2001 McCrimmon Publishing Co. Ltd.

ISBN 0 85597 632 2

Illustrations © Wllllam Webb
Design and layout by Nick Snode

Typeset in Georgia 12pt and Textile 22pt
Printed on 115gsn Fineblade coated art
Printed and bound by Thanet Press, Margate, Kent

Introducing children to our faith

God is Love.

Conception and giving birth are both acts of love.

When your child first received your love, they encountered God.

You brought them into the presence of God.

Your child did not meet God for the first time in church.

Faith starts with life. Faith does not start with a set of statements or a list of rules.

Whenever we enter the mystery of life and creation we encounter God.

There is so much in life that words cannot fully explain, such as love -

> We recognise:

> "There is more to life than meets the eye".

> Faith does not attempt to explain the mystery of life
> rather it helps us to enter into the mystery and participate in it.

> God is the Mystery.

Passing on a sense of wonder

Spend some moments with your child:

star gazing;
watching birds fly;
watching rain, snow, hail, wind
and their effects;
watching running water. *

listening to instrumental music;
listening to birds singing;
listening to the wind. *

hugging each other;
stroking animals;
playing in water;
playing in sand. *

mixing paints, watching yellow and
blue turn green;
planting seeds;
picking flowers. *

aware of the scent of flowers;
of food cooking,
and other smells. *

reading stories and
poems to them *

bring your child's attention
to their growth, whenever they
need new clothes *

Prayer   * and say:

Glory be to God

or

Praise be to God

Pass on to your children:

a sense of wonder,

a desire to ask questions.

Called by Name

When your child was brought for Baptism you were asked, "What name do you give this child?" A name is one of the first gifts you give your daughter or son.

What is your full name?   *Where did it come from?*

What family names have you?

Think back...

    What was your mother's maiden name?

    What were your grandmothers' maiden names?

Which family names have been forgotten?   *Some day,*

Which family names have been remembered?   *tell the children*

Who was special?   *in your family.*

What is the nicest name anyone has ever called you?

    A nick name,   *These are the names*

    a pet name,   *by which we are known*

    an intimate name?   *by God.*

What name have you given your child?   Why did you choose this name?

Passing on some names for God

God our Father

Tender God   Welcoming God

God of worries   Sleeping God   Comforting God

Dancing God   God of energy

God of change   Gentle God   God of understanding

God who weeps   God of hope

God of good dreams   Healing God   Brave God

God of surprises   Smiling God

Mysterious God   Laughing God

Waiting God   God who knows sadness   Excited God

God who knows failure   Caring God

God our Mother

Prayer   Choose a name, from above and ask for God's blessing on each family member.

Use your own names for God too.

Pass on to your children:

the importance of respecting names

Jesus

If we want to know God in human terms we have a complete picture in Jesus. To know Jesus is to know God.

For us to be familiar with Jesus we need to be familiar with the scriptures. The place of the Bible in the Catholic faith cannot be overestimated. A good starting point is one of the four gospels.

Gospel means Good News.

What is the good news made known to us through Jesus?

We are all equally loved by God
even though we sin.
God has no favourites.

Our sin is forgiven
we are invited to receive God's forgiveness
and live in peace.

We can live life in all its fullness now.

Jesus shows us the way.

The Good News, 'God is Love' is for everyone! It is not complicated.

– Matthew chapter 11, verses 25 and 26 –

**At that time Jesus exclaimed, 'I bless you, Father, Lord of heaven and of earth, for hiding these things from the learned and the clever and revealing them to mere children.
Yes, Father, for that is what it pleases you to do.'**

Passing on some stories of Jesus

Children's first introduction to the Bible should be seeing it in the hands of their parents or other important adults.
It should be read to them before they read it for themselves.

 Choose Bibles that you can both enjoy.

Some

 When reading the Bible to children help them to imagine they are part of the story, perhaps pretending to be a character.

suggestions

to consider... Ask for help at church especially from anyone involved in 'Liturgy of the Word with Children'.

 Television companies often screen stories about Jesus. "Story Keepers" (ITV) is particularly popular with children and adults alike. Watch these together.

Footnote: The Bible is really a library with many books. There are 75 pieces of writing altogether written in the course of many centuries. It includes all sorts of texts, history, poetry, stories, legends and so on. We need to understand a little of what we are reading. When choosing books with passages from the Bible, choose ones on the basis of the usefulness of the explanations they give rather than their illustrations. If none are available as a rough guide read the passages as you would poetry. They carry truth which is not always expressed literally.

The Cross

During a baptism the priest traces a cross on the child's forehead and then invites the parents and godparents to do the same.
The child is "marked with the sign of faith." Why?

The Cross reminds us

Just as Jesus is with us when we are happy,
he is also with us when we are sad.

"We are glad to have his company!"

Little in life is entirely good or bad.
Sorrow and joy are the two sides of the same coin.
In life we meet all sorts of problems and see people we love suffer.

As Christians we do not pretend that suffering does not exist.
Jesus knew suffering and sorrow: temptation, betrayal and a sense of being abandoned.
He suffered a cruel death at the hands of the people of his day.

This cruel death was not at God's request.
God's response was to raise Jesus to new life.

Suffering and death are very real to us but we can see beyond them,
they are not the end for us,
they do not have the last word.

Passing on the sign of the Cross

Buy a cross or crucifix (a cross with the figure of Jesus) or ask your child's godparents to give your child one as a baptismal gift.

During difficult times:

Touch the cross

Make the sign of the cross

Prayer

Whenever your child is facing a difficult time trace the cross on their forehead saying,
(in these or similar words)

May God give you strength today

or

May God be with you

and perhaps kiss their forehead.

Pass on to your children:

Our faith is that we always have hope,

suffering does not have the last word.

Dignity

What gives you your dignity?

For Christians, your dignity comes from being made in the image and likeness of God and from the love lavished on you by God.
We are all God's children whether we are christian or not.

Our dignity is damaged only by sin – sin is not treating ourselves or others, with the dignity proper to children of God.

Baptism celebrates the christian belief that we are loved by God.
It also acknowledges that the world is sinful and that we are all too easily caught up in its influences and attractions.
During the ceremony promises to say no to sin and selfishness are made and water is poured over the baby (or adult) as a sign of God's love and forgiveness.

Though time and time again we continue to behave sinfully we are nevertheless children of God. We struggle, not on our own but with the whole Church to ensure our dignity and that of others is recognised.
Baptism celebrates our choice to be part of this Christian family, the Church.

God continues to love and offer forgiveness to all.

Towards the end of the ceremony

As a sign of their dignity, the child (or adult) being baptised is clothed or wrapped in a white garment, often a shawl.

Wrapped in the love of their parent
Wrapped in the love of their family
Wrapped in the love of the community
Wrapped in the love of God
who is deeply in love with this child.

You are a child of God
Your child is a child of God
Their birth proclaims it
Baptism celebrates it!
Your child's dignity is recognised.

Teach your children to:

have a positive image of themselves no matter what others may say;

forgive themselves;

have a positive image of others;

forgive others;

seek all that is good and true.

Help your child to experience God's love and guide them in the way of Jesus; love of God, our neighbour and ourselves.

21

Candles

One of the last gifts given during a baptism is a candle.
It is usually given with the words, "Parents and Godparents,
this light is entrusted to you to be kept burning brightly".

Children love candles, they recognise that they are somehow special.

For yourselves:

Light a candle

Look at the light.

How do you feel?

Think of a word that
describes how you are feeling.

Describe your feelings.

Blow out the light

How do you feel?

Choose a word that
describes your feelings.

Passing on the light of Jesus

Relight the candle

– From the Gospel of St John, chapter 12, verse 46 –

**Jesus said,
I, the light have come into the world
so that whoever believes in me
need not stay in the dark anymore.**

Enjoy the feeling it gives you.
Spend a moment in silence.

Prayer

* Light a candle for a minute or so a day
  always on   Sundays
                 Birthdays
                 other celebrations

* Light it whenever you want
  to be conscious of the
  presence of Jesus when
  you want his company

* After your moments of
  silence say to those present,

  'Peace be with you'.

Pass on to your children:

*The joy and peace of knowing the
presence of Jesus with you*

Blessings

Blessings are not good luck charms, a way of getting special favours, nor are they about becoming God's favourites.
God has no favourites, everyone is loved by God, unconditionally.

Blessings are gifts

and the giver, God,

delights in seeing us use his gifts.

At the end of the baptism the mother, father and everyone gathered are blessed.

There are three blessings, gifts to be shared with your child.

First blessing:

✳ **Gifts of Hope of eternal life and thanksgiving**

Second blessing:

✳ **Gifts of Teaching and Witnessing**

Final blessing:

✳ **Gifts of Faith and Peace, and much more**

Passing on blessings

Unwrap the gifts for your children

* **Hope of eternal life and thanksgiving**

    Open your eyes and your child's eyes to all that is good
    and give thanks for the good you see.

    God did not create us to turn us away,
    our lives will change in death, not end.
    All that is good lasts for ever.

* **Teaching and Witnessing**

    Stand up for what is right and true.

* **Faith and Peace**

    Keep your child company in their journey of faith and
     introduce them to other children and people in church.

    Work through difficult times with your child.
    Discover all that is good and true.

Prayer   (Ask for God's blessings by name)

May God bless us with all good things

     (e.g. peace, friendship, patience, happiness, courage, laughter...)

so that we can show we are truly God's friends.
   Amen.

Introducing some Church rituals

Baptism is full of ritual. Here are some rituals to introduce to your child in their early years which will help them to feel at home in church.

Lighting candles.

Genuflecting before the presence of Jesus in the tabernacle in church.

Joining hands when praying.

Blessing themselves by dipping their fingers in holy water and then making the sign of the cross.

Familiarising children with the church building

When you think they are old enough take them into church if possible when there is no service taking place.

As the months and years go by, gradually let your child seek out:

something shiny
something big
something small

then later as they get older:

something special
something lovely to look at
somewhere lovely to be

and older,   something about Jesus

and older,   something that tells
them about the people who come to this church

something that tells something about what
they do when they are here

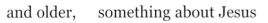

Let them freely walk about on these visits seeking out for themselves.

Point out your choices to the above.

The First letter of John

Something which has existed since the beginning,

that we have heard,

and we have seen with our own eyes;

that we have watched

and touched with our hands:

the Word, who is life –

this is our subject.

That life was made visible:

we saw it and we are giving our testimony,

telling you of the eternal life

which was with the Father and has been made visible to us.

What we have seen and heard

we are telling you

so that you too may be in union with us,

as we are in union

with the Father

and with his Son Jesus Christ.

We are writing this to you to make our own joy complete.

1 John, chapter 1, verses 1 to 4